Jamie.

Have a great one

all the best

Andrew

So You're
40!

Mike Haskins & Clive Whichelow

summersdale

SO YOU'RE 40!

Summersdale Publishers Ltd
46 West Street
Chichester
West Sussex
PO19 1RP
UK

www.summersdale.com

Printed and bound in China

ISBN 13: 978-1-84024-562-2

INTRODUCTION

So you've made it! You're in your forties! Congratulations!

Finally, you're a proper grown-up.

OK, in many parts of the world and at many previous ages in history, 40 would represent your total life expectancy.

But don't worry about those doom-mongers who tell you it's all downhill physically and mentally from now on. What the hell do those so-called fully qualified doctors and other medical experts know anyway?

And don't worry that deep down inside you know you haven't really matured one iota since you were fifteen.

Life, they say, begins at 40. Obviously that's blatantly untrue. But it is a thing people (often around the age of 40) say to one another.

You've got everything to look forward to, they say. Obviously that's blatantly untrue as well. Realistically speaking you've got about half of everything to look forward to.

But seeing as you've reached 40 without anything much ever happening to you, you can now get on with the best half of your life armed with this little book – the ideal primer to what is surely destined to be the greatest decade of your entire life.

THE BASIC MYTHS ABOUT TURNING 40

Life begins – well your sex life certainly doesn't.

Maturity has at last made you a fount of knowledge and wisdom – what a pity no one's the least bit interested in listening to you any more.

You're now at an age when young people will flock to you and look up to you with awe and respect – this will only happen if you're their drug dealer.

You'll be at the peak of your career – this is hard to believe when you're stuck in a dull, dead-end office job surrounded by idiots.

Now you're 40 you have the face you deserve – if so, I'd demand a retrial.

THINGS YOU WILL NEVER NOW DO

Become a rock star

Regain the waist size you had
when you were 18

Regain the ability to bite your own toenails

Grow out of your problems

DRESS CODE FOR THE OVER 40s – SOME DO'S & DON'TS

Do learn to laugh at yourself – at least you can beat everyone else to it.

Don't turn to transvestism at this stage of your life – it will only emphasise any problems you have.

Don't try and squeeze into any trousers
you have owned for more than two years
– not only will you look ridiculous, there
will also be a significant chance
of asphyxiation.

Don't think anyone wants
to see your midriff.

TIPS ON HOW TO LOOK YOUNGER THAN YOU ACTUALLY ARE

Learn to send a text message in less than twenty minutes.

Attach a very large bulldog clip to the back of your head to help smooth out all the wrinkles.

Buy a load of new clothes from a really trendy shop then wear the bag over your head.

Avoid the following: all-night parties, drinking, drugs, one-night stands... or basically all the things young people do.

GIVEAWAYS THAT WILL TELL PEOPLE YOU ARE OVER 40

You end text messages with
'Yours sincerely'.

When someone asks you to a burn a CD,
you reach for the matches.

You complain about graffiti.

A GUIDE TO HOW OTHERS WILL NOW PERCEIVE YOU

By old ladies at bus stops as someone who is not so likely to nick their bag

By small children as someone who remembers World War Two

By older people as someone who now agrees with their more extreme opinions

As a source of pocket money

CULTURE CONVERTER

When speaking with people younger than yourself it's no use talking about things that happened before they were born, they won't have a clue what you're on about. So here is a handy culture converter to translate your cultural reference points to their equivalent:

Category	Your Age	People Who Are Still Old But Irritatingly Younger Than You	Young People	Very Young People
Pop/rock band	U2	Oasis	McFly	The Tweenies
Heart-throb	Simon Le Bon	Robbie Williams	Justin Timberlake	Bob the Builder
Pin-up	Samantha Fox	Melinda Messenger	Jordan	Barbie
Daft fashion	New Romantic kilt	Acid house baby's dummy	Hoodie	Baby's dummy (for more obvious reasons)
Football hero	Kevin Keegan	Gary Lineker	David Beckham	Wayne Rooney

THE MAIN THINGS IN YOUR LIFE YOU WILL NOW LOOK FORWARD TO

Going to see your favourite band who have come back on a reunion tour

No longer having to stay in fashion

No longer having your libido dictate
your every decision in life

And best of all – only ten years now till
you can book a Saga holiday!

THE MAIN THINGS IN YOUR LIFE IT'S LESS EASY TO LOOK FORWARD TO

Going to see your favourite band who have come back on a reunion tour and realising you didn't actually like them that much at the time

The first time someone just assumes you have children

The first time clothes from your youth
come back into fashion

The first time your children announce
they've been studying something that
happened in your lifetime in the
history lesson at school

CONVERSING WITH YOUNG PEOPLE (PART 1)

What you say and what they hear

'OK, kids. Who wants a game of football?' = 'Let me show off in front of you and your friends for ten minutes before I keel over and lie on the ground gasping for breath.'

'How did your exams go?' = 'Let me tell you how much harder exams were in my day.'

'So, what sort of music do you like?' = 'I desperately need to find out what's cool because I'm completely out of touch with what's going on.'

STATISTICALLY SPEAKING

If you're 40 you have lived around
14,610 days or 2,087 weeks.

If you've managed to get a decent
night's sleep of seven hours each night,
you have so far spent 12.5 years
of your life just lying there
snoring and dribbling.

If you have watched an average of 2.5 hours' television a day since you were four, this would represent over 3.75 years of your entire life spent plonked in front of the box.

If you have spent £20 a week on alcohol since your eighteenth birthday, to date you have wasted almost £23,000 giving yourself hangovers. If you've spent eight hours a week in the pub that would represent an entire year of your life.

If you've been in full-time employment since you were 21, you will have spent over six years of your life at work – if you've spent an hour and a half each day getting to and from work that's another entire year gone.

So if you've spent 12.5 years sleeping, 3.75 years watching TV, 1 year in the pub, 6 years at work and 1 year getting to work, your actual life has so far lasted only 15.75 years – happy 15.75th birthday!

NOW YOU'RE 40 THE FOLLOWING WILL BE YOUR NATURAL ENEMIES

Next door's cat

Anyone in a bigger car than yours

Gravity

A LIST OF CONTROVERSIAL OPINIONS YOU WILL NOW BE LIKELY TO HOLD

'They should bring back the workhouse/ national service/birching/Mrs Thatcher.'

'Anyone caught wearing a baseball cap while at the wheel of a car should be stripped of their licence.'

'The police should be entitled to use Tasers on anyone who swears in a public place.'

CONVERSING WITH YOUNG PEOPLE (PART 2)

What they say and what you hear

'Mummy/Daddy! Will you have a game on the PlayStation with me?' = 'Mummy/Daddy! Can I thrash you on the PlayStation?'

'Mummy/Daddy! Where do babies come from?' = 'Mummy/Daddy! I'd like to watch you squirm with embarrassment for the next ten minutes.'

'Trick or treat' = 'Give me some sweets or me and Dracula here'll mug you.

'Daddy, who were those funny ladies you were looking at on the computer?' = 'Daddy, would you like to consider putting my pocket money up a bit?'

THINGS YOU CAN NOW GET AWAY WITH THAT YOU COULDN'T PREVIOUSLY

Pulling the bin out to the front
of your house while only
dressed in your pyjamas

Talking to an 18-year-old without them thinking you're trying to chat them up

Feigning a mild heart attack to gain an advantage during a family dispute

THINGS YOU SHOULD HAVE
ACHIEVED BY NOW

Being able to say 'Uranus' without
giggling and making a puerile joke

Wearing sunglasses only when it's sunny

The ability to change a washer
in one of your taps

The ability to have a good time
regardless of how miserable the rest of
your family are looking during a day out

THINGS YOU ARE NOW LIKELY TO HAVE IN YOUR HOME

A copy of *The National Trust Handbook*

A wine rack (moreover, one that is not permanently empty)

The registration number of every vehicle to
have parked illegally outside your house

A packet of moist toilet tissue

THINGS THAT YOU WILL TAKE A SUDDEN INTEREST IN

The fact that the BBC also has Radios 2, 3 and 4

Adverts containing the words 'younger', 'rejuvenate' and 'free'

Your cholesterol level

The best route by road from your house
to anywhere else in the country

THINGS YOU'LL FEEL
SMUG ABOUT

Still having 20/20 vision

The amount you recycle compared to the
amount next door have sticking out of
the top of their wheelie bin

Being old enough to remember the
'Hurricane of '87'

Making it through the night without
having to get up and go to the toilet

HOORAY! THINGS YOU'LL NEVER HAVE TO DO AGAIN

Eat the hottest curry in the restaurant – with extra chillies

Sleep in a muddy field at Glastonbury

Pretend to get high on a joint made out of Earl Grey tea and bran flakes

BOO! THINGS YOU WON'T BE DOING AGAIN

Admiring your body in a full-length mirror (a full-width mirror might be more like it)

Wondering who your Valentine's Day cards are from

Loving them and leaving them (you will not have the energy to do both)

Attending rock concerts without feeling just a little bit self-conscious

SHATTERING MOMENTS TO COME SOON

Your first grey hair

A politician who is younger than you

Your first grey pubic hair

A prime minister who is
younger than you

Realising many people born in the 1980s
are now in full-time employment, some
of them earning significantly
more than you do

THINGS TO EXPECT FOR YOUR NEXT BIRTHDAY

Some worthless object made by one of your children

A supposedly amusing book about life in your forties

A hand-knitted jumper

BEING 40 IS...

... being too old for nightclubs but too young for nightcaps.

... being too old for hair gel but too young for hair dye.

... being too old to be hip and too young for a hip replacement.

... being too old to be looked after by your parents and too young to be looked after by your kids – you're on your own, mate!

THINGS YOU SHOULD NOT HAVE IN YOUR HOME

Your own superhero outfit (no – not even a crotchless one)

Love letters from all your exes

A whoopee cushion/talking toilet roll holder/pretend dog poo

AARGHH! THINGS YOU NEVER THOUGHT WOULD HAPPEN

You get asked to play for a veterans' sports team.

Your new boss is younger than you.

You have finally turned into
your mum/dad.

You have regular sessions with a
physiotherapist/chiropractor/shrink.

YOUR NEW OUTLOOK
ON LIFE

Your idea of a busy weekend is doing the
shopping and washing the car.

Your idea of rebellion is refusing to
have a shop loyalty card.

Your idea of life in the fast lane is queuing at the 'Five items or fewer' checkout in the supermarket.

YOUR NEW WEEKLY
HIGHLIGHTS

Going to the bottle bank

Buying a new plant for the garden

Seeing what free CD comes with
the Sunday paper

THINGS YOU WILL DESPERATELY TRY TO AVOID

Going up yet another jeans size

Admitting you need to sit down in the pub

Wearing glasses

THOSE WERE THE DAYS! NOSTALGIA FOR THE OVER 40s

When STD was a new telephone system

When a chat room was the
front bar of the local pub

When a happy slapper was a girl who
enjoyed herself a lot

When a mobile was what you had
hanging from your bedroom ceiling

THINGS YOU SHOULD NO LONGER HAVE IN YOUR CAR

Fluffy dice/nodding dogs/cute cuddly
toys – you're supposed to
be a grown-up!

Underwear belonging to someone whose
name you can no longer remember

An aggressive rear-window sticker – You can only get away with 'Back off – bitch driving' when you're 22

A driving instructor

THINGS YOU WON'T BE DOING ON HOLIDAY ANY MORE

Wearing a swimsuit only slightly larger than an elastic band

Being drunk in charge of a windsurfboard

Putting your head out of your hotel door without being daubed with factor 1,000,000 sun cream

REASONS TO
BE CHEERFUL

You're no longer defined by what
trainers you wear.

Despite the extraordinary amount of
environmental damage wreaked on it,
planet earth will probably just about
see you out now.

You're mature at last – and if anyone
disagrees you'll give them
a Chinese burn.